My Mat!

By Cameron Macintosh

Sam is at the mat.

It is Tam.

Tam taps the mat.

Sam sits.

Tam sits.

CHECKING FOR MEANING

1. Who sits on the mat first? *(Literal)*

2. Who wants to sit on the mat? *(Literal)*

3. Do you think Sam and Tam came up with a good solution to their problem? *(Inferential)*

EXTENDING VOCABULARY

sits	How many sounds are in the word *sits*? How many letters? Can you find another word in the book with four sounds?
taps	Find the word *taps* in the book. What is the base of *taps*? Can you find the base in the book?
is	Look at the word *is*. What sound does the letter *s* make in this word? What sound does *s* make in *Sam*?

MOVING BEYOND THE TEXT

1. When have you had to share something with someone else?

2. What can you do to be a good friend?

3. How can you solve problems that you might have with your friends?

4. Where else might you find a mat?

SPEED SOUNDS

Mm	Ss	Aa	Pp	Ii	Tt

PRACTICE WORDS

at

mat

Sam

Tam

taps

It

Tap

sits

tap